The Chronicles of Bumblebania

A Bumble Christmas Carol

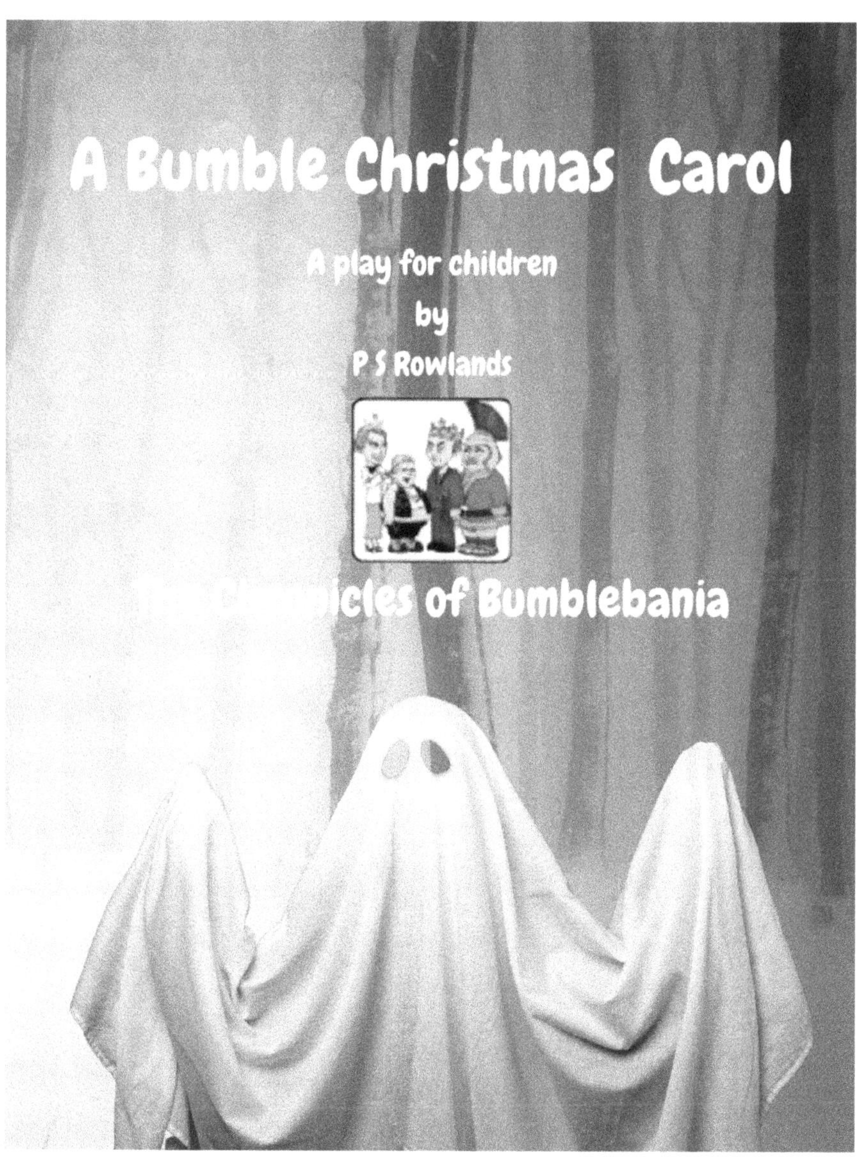

By

P S Rowlands

Reproduction Rights

SCENE 1: INT. WIZARD FUMBLE'S COTTAGE

FX:	**WIZARD FUMBLE IS READING THE 'BUMBLEBANIA CHRONICLE WHILE HIS WIFE SITS OPPOSITE HIM KNITTING A SCARF.**
FUMBLE:	This is the last straw! The straw that broke the camel's back.
WIFE:	What's that dear? The camel's back? I didn't know it had gone anywhere.
FUMBLE:	I meant, oh, never mind. It's bad enough that Aunt Grimwalda has invited herself for a visit again. The neighbours still haven't forgiven us for the last time.
WIFE:	You can't blame Auntie. "*A wagon full of toys*" does sound awfully like "*a dragon full of boys*."
FUMBLE:	You have a point, I suppose, dear. I must admit, it is quieter these days. Anyway, it's not Auntie I'm annoyed with.
WIFE:	It's not?
FUMBLE:	No, it's the King—old skinflint himself.
WIFE:	What's he done now? Put a tax on piggy banks?
FUMBLE:	He did that last week, but he's gone too far this time. He's banned Christmas.
WIFE:	Banned Christmas! But why? Christmas is a time of joy: baby Jesus in the manger, the smiling faces of little

children, plum pudding, Christmas stockings, and presents.

FUMBLE: Presents, exactly!

WIFE: He's too mean to buy any, but what can we do? He is the King, the rightful ruler of Bumblebania, unfortunately.

FUMBLE Never fear, I've an idea..

WIFE: I hope it's a good one. I always feel nervous when you break into rhyme Fumble.

FUMBLE: I read this book once about a miser called Scrooge. He was almost as mean as the King.

WIFE: I don't believe it.

FUMBLE: I did say 'almost', dear.

WIFE: What happened to this Scrooge person?

FUMBLE: He was visited by three Spirits.

WIFE: Oh no, Fumble, you wouldn't? You would! Ghosts, how exciting!

SCENE 2: INT. THE PALACE

FX: **KING BUMBLE IS SAT AT A TABLE SURROUNDED BY PILES OF COINS. HE IS WRITING IN A LEDGER. SIR BORIS STANDS BY THE FIRE DANGLING USED TEABAGS OVER THE FLAMES.**

KING: When you've finished drying those teabags, Boris, you can fetch more logs for the fire.

BORIS: But Sire, it's a long way to the forest, it's snowing and I've got a hole in my slippers. And what about the wolves?

KING: Wolves? Don't be ridiculous, Boris. There are no Wolves in Bumblebania. The odd bear or two, perhaps, but with luck, you shouldn't run into any of them. They'll be too busy hunting for food. Ravenous by now, I shouldn't wonder. Well, off you go, Boris.

BORIS: But Sire.

KING: Come on, Boris, where's your Christmas spirit?

BORIS: You've banned it, Sire.

KING: Boris OUT!

FX: **BORIS TROOPS FORLORNLY OUT OF THE ROOM PASSING BARON GRIME ON THE WAY.**

KING: Baron Grime, what do you want?

BARON: Merry Christmas, Your Majesty, I mean, festive greetings. Lovely day isn't it?

KING: What do you want, Baron? Can't you see I'm busy with my accounts? I have a funny feeling that '*The Sunrise Home for Homeless Knights*' hasn't sent me enough taxes. Well, speak up.

BARON: I'm collecting for charity, Your Majesty.

KING: That's very thoughtful of you, Baron.

FX: KING BUMBLE STANDS AND HOLDS OUT HIS HANDS EXPECTANTLY.

BARON: Not for you, Sire, it's for the B.B.B.F.

FX: KING BUMBLE SITS DOWN AND GLARES AT BARON GRIME.

KING: The what?

BARON: The, um, '*Battered Barons Benevolent Fund*', Your Majesty.

KING: Battered Barons? If I had my way, they'd be mashed Barons, bashed Barons, thrashed Barons, outcast Barons.

FX: KING BUMBLE GETS TO HIS FEET AS BARON GRIME GINGERLY BACKS AWAY.

Do I make myself clear? Good day, Baron!

FX: BARON GRIME SLINKS OFF AS THE CHANCELLOR ENTERS HESITANTLY.

CHANCELLOR: Excuse me, Your Majesty.

KING: What is it, Chancellor? Can't you see I'm busy counting my money?

FX: THE KING SHAKES A PIGGY BANK IN THE CHANCELLORS FACE.

CHANCELLOR: It's the Queen, Your Majesty.

KING: The Queen? She's not back, is she? She should be visiting her sister until next January. Quick Chancellor, fetch the artificial Christmas from the attic. Where's Boris? Boris!

CHANCELLOR: She's not back, Sire.

KING: Don't dawdle, man, this is an emergency. . . not back, not back? Then what on earth are you talking about?

FX: THE CHANCELLOR PRODUCES A LETTER AND HANDS IT TO THE KING

CHANCELLOR: A letter, Sire. From the Queen.

KING: Why didn't you say so in the first place? You're becoming lax of late, Chancellor, very lax. It won't do. It won't do at all. From now on, Chancellor, I'm halving your salary.

CHANCELLOR: You can't, Sire/

KING: Can't, what do you mean can't? I'm the King, and you're my subject. I'd chop your head off for your cheek if I could afford a Royal Executioner. Why can't I?

CHANCELLOR: Because you don't pay me any wages, Sire.

KING: Don't I? Very sensible. Well, Chancellor, you can consider yourself lucky that I don't; otherwise, you'd have them halved. So there!

CHANCELLOR: Is there anything else, Your Majesty?

KING: No. Wait a moment. If you happen to see Sir Boris, tell him not to carry too many logs on his back

CHANCELLOR: That's very thoughtful of Your Majesty. Boris's back has been giving him trouble lately.

KING: Of course, poor chap. None of us getting any younger. Tell him not to worry, Chancellor. He can make two journeys.

CHANCELLOR: Your Majesty is kindness itself.

KING: Well, come on, man, read the letter.

CHANCELLOR: *"Dear Bumble, I hope you are managing in my absence and not forgetting to wear your night socks."*

KING: Of course, I'm wearing my night socks – er, managing. Does the Queen think I'm an idiot or something?

CHANCELLOR: Her Majesty isn't specific on that point, Sire.

KING: What? Get on with it, Chancellor.

CHANCELLOR: *"Whatever you do, dear, don't let things go to your head."*

KING: "*Things go to my head?*" As if I would. Anyway, I'm the King. I can do what I like. Anybody would think I'm not up to the job.

CHANCELLOR: *"And remember to eat your greens."*

KING: Of course, dear, I mean. . . That will be all for now, Chancellor. Off you go. Time is money.

CHANCELLOR: And *"Rupert sends his love."* Good day, Sire.

FX: THE CHANCELLOR EXITS

KING: Did he have to mention that name? I think I am starting to have a headache. Doctor! Doctor!

FX: THE COURT JESTER ENTERS

JESTER: Hello, hello, hello. Did you hear about the Englishman the. . .

KING: Doctor?

JESTER: No, not the doctor, the Englishman, the. . .

KING: Shut up! I want the doctor.

JESTER: I am the doctor and the carpenter, and the plumber, and the cook, and the. . .

KING: Alright, never mind all that. I've got a headache, and I want you to cure it.

<u>FX: THE COURT JESTER PLACES ONE HAND ON THE KINGS BROW WHILE THE OTHER CHECKS THE KING'S PULSE.</u>

JESTER: Hmmmm! Yes, I see.

KING: What is it?

JESTER: Hot flushes.

KING: Is there anything you can do?

JESTER: I could drain your tank.

KING: Oh, shut up. I'm going to bed. Chancellor put out the fire. No point wasting heat.

SCENE 3: EXT. THE LONELY FOREST

FX: **BARON GRIME CAUTIOUSLY APPROACHES WHAT APPEARS TO BE A SNOWMAN IN THE MIDDLE OF THE WOODS.**

BARON: What a place to build a snowman. Strange, I seem to recognise those features. Fat, flabby chin, loose lower lip, shifty eyes. . . it can't be!

BORIS: Aaaatishoooo!.

BARON: A sneezing snowman? It must be. . . Boris, is that you?

BORIS: Of ccccourse it's mmmmeee.

BARON: I thought even you would have more sense than to play games out here in the middle of nowhere, in the forest, Boris.

BORIS: Ggggames? This is no ggggame, you know, Baron.

BARON: Oh, I see. Just waiting for a bus, eh, Boris?

BORIS: Actually, I'm in ttttraining.

BARON: Ttttraining? They don't have standing-still races in the Olympics, Boris,

BORIS: I'm not training for the Olympics; I'm training to be a snowman.

BARON: Poor chap, I knew it was inevitable. He always was feeble-minded. Now his brain's collapsed completely.

BORIS: You don't understand Bbbbaron. This is ccccamouflage.

BARON: Ccccamouflage?

BORIS: Aaaatishoooo! Exactly, Baron, ccccamouflage.

BARON: But why a snowman, Boris?

BORIS: Obvious to anyone, I'd have thought.

BARON: It may be obvious to another snowman, Boris. But would you please enlighten me?

BORIS: I'm setting a trap.

BARON: A trap, what for, fugitive flakes? Ha, ha, ha.

BORIS: The Abominable Snowman, of course. Aaaatishoooo!

BARON: How do you intend to catch the Snowman, Boris, by giving him influenza?

BORIS: I wouldn't dream of resorting to anything as dastardly as biological warfare, Baron. Not like some people I could mention. By my brilliant impersonation, I shall lure the beast back to a specially prepared cave.

BARON: Oh, shut up, Boris. You don't think I'm going to be taken in by such childish claptrap. My name's Grime, not Bumble.

BORIS: Claptrap! I'll show you. . . aaaatishoooo!

BARON: Yes, Boris, CLAPTRAP! I don't believe a word of it, and neither do you. Come on, show me how you intend to lure the Abominable Snowman back to the cave.

FX: BORIS STRUGGLES TO MOVE A FROZEN MUSCLE BUT ONLY SUCCEEDS IN GETTING REDDER IN THE FACE.

BORIS: Show you? I'll show you, alright.

BARON: You seem to be having a little trouble moving.

BORIS: (STILL STRUGGLING) A little stiff, perhaps.

BARON: Stiff, ha! You're as frozen as a fish finger. I hope dear old A.B. doesn't like his meat straight from the deep freeze.

FX: BARON GRIME TURNS TO WALK AWAY.

BORIS: I say, Baron, old chap, don't leave me here alone in the forest.

BARON: Well, I suppose it is Christmas, after all.

BORIS: That's the spirit Baron. . . Christmas cheer. . . jingle bells . . . Good King Wenceslas and all that.

BARON: No, sorry, Boris, King's orders. You, of all people, should know that he's banned Christmas.

BORIS: Please, Baron, I'll let you play with my X-Box Christmas morning. I mean December the 25th.

BARON: All day?

BORIS: Shan't!

BARON: Goodbye, Boris. I think I'll be getting off home. It's almost time for my cocoa. Besides, it's getting dark, and they say that apart from bears, wolves, and abominable snowmen, the forest is haunted.

FX: BARON GRIME TURNS TO WALK AWAY.

BORIS: Wait a sec, Baron. I was only kidding. Of course, you can borrow my Xbox.

BARON: Right, Boris. Let's swear our solemn oath. No crossed fingers, mind. One. . . two. . . three. . .

TOGETHER: If I break this oath today.
May my toenails fade away.
If tomorrow I may stray,
No more sweeties come my way.

FX: BARON GRIME MASSAGES BORIS' FROZEN ARMS UNTIL HE IS ABLE TO MOVE. BORIS SHUFFLES AFTER THE BARON, WHO PAUSES AND POINTS AT A PILE OF WOOD.

BARON: By the way, Boris, don't forget your sticks.

FX: BORIS BENDS OVER TO PICK UP THE FIREWOOD.

BORIS: Oh no, thanks, Baron. . . oh!

BARON: It's alright, Boris. I know that old skinflint Bumble sent you out to fetch firewood. It's disgraceful how he treats you, the bravest, most revered knight in the Kingdom.

BORIS: True, true, I can't deny it. I am the bravest knight in the Realm. Did you hear how I . . .

BARON: Not now, Boris, later perhaps. The old Scrooge even refused to contribute to the B.B.B.F.

BORIS: The B.B.B.F., what's that?

BARON: The Battered Barons Benevolent Fund. I don't suppose you'd like to contribute, Boris?

BORIS: (PRODUCING A NOTE FROM HIS POCKET) I haven't anything smaller than this note, I'm afraid.

BARON: (SNATCHING IT FROM BORIS' GRASP) Thank you Boris. Very generous, I'm sure.

BORIS: I've never heard of the B.B.B.F. Have you many dependents, Baron?

BARON: Just the one at the moment, me. But we're hoping to expand in the near future.

BORIS: I see. We knights have a fund as well, you know.

BARON: Sorry, Boris, I'm right out of change. But we're wasting time standing here. Listen, something has to be done about the King. He's growing meaner by the minute. I'm on my way to meet Wizard Fumble. He has a plan.

BORIS: Fumble? Do you think that's wise, Baron? The old chap's a bit unstable, to say the least.

BARON: That's why I asked you, Boris. I knew the most courageous, daring, bold knight in the Kingdom wouldn't be afraid to risk meeting with Wizard Fumble.

FX: DEEP IN THE FOREST A CREATURE HOWLS.

BORIS: What's that?

BOTH: Wolves! Heeeeelp!

FX: THE BARON AND BORIS FLEE INTO THE FOREST.

SCENE 4. INT. WIZARD FUMBLE'S COTTAGE

FX: **WIZARD FUMBLE PACES BACK AND FORTH WHILE HIS WIFE SITS QUIETLY KNITTING**

WIFE: Sit down, dear. You'll wear your wand out if you keep waving it about like that. You've changed the cat into a mouse three times already. I don't know how to get him out from behind the skirting.

FUMBLE: I do wish they'd hurry up.

WIFE: Fumble, remember you promised. No more wishes till we find the milkman.

FUMBLE: Don't nag, Beloved. That was three Christmases ago. Besides, I had a cold at the time. He's probably reappeared somewhere by now.

FX: **BANG! BANG! BANG! THREE LOUD KNOCKS ON THE DOOR**

WIFE: Come in before you break the door down.

FX: **BARON GRIME AND SIR BORIS STUMBLE INSIDE.**

FUMBLE: Baron, I thought you'd never get here. Stop! Don't move. (WHISPERING) Do you know you've been followed?

BARON: Followed? Who, what, where?

FUMBLE: Behind you. An evil-looking creature if ever I saw one. (POINTING HIS WAND AT SIR BORIS) Don't panic, Baron. I'll soon get rid of him.

BORIS: I say, Baron. Why is Wizard Fumble pointing his wand at me?

BARON: Wait! Don't shoot. It's alright, Fumble, he's with me. He's a friend.

WIZARD: Who is he?

BARON: Sir Boris, the famous knight errant. Boris the Bold?

FUMBLE: Oh, him, why is he grovelling on the floor?

BARON: Boris, why are you grovelling?

BORIS: Grovelling, me? Is that what it looks like? I'm just checking for tracks, you know, Baron. As you say, Wizard Fumble, we may have been followed. Can't be too careful, you know.

WIFE: Tell him to get up, Fumble. He'll frighten the cat.

FUMBLE: I could turn him into a toad.

WIFE: For the last time, Fumble, put that wand away and tell him to get up.

FUMBLE: Get up! What did you want to bring him for Baron?

BARON: Because he's just as fed up with the old skinflint as we are. He's willing to do practically anything to get rid of him.

BORIS: Anything? I say, Baron, old chap, I wouldn't go quite that far. Well, that is to say, I am jolly annoyed, you know.

BARON: Shut up, Boris. Well, Fumble, have you thought of a plan yet?

FUMBLE: Thought of a plan? I'll say I have.

In a castle on a hill,
There lives a King so stingy,
His subjects walk about in rags,
Because he is so mingy.

WIFE: Fumble!

WIZARD: Don't worry dear, it's only a short one. Where was I?

BORIS: "Mingy".

WIZARD: Ah yes,

His treasure house is full of gold,
He really is quite wealthy,
And yet his vest is full of holes.
I'm sure it isn't healthy.

BORIS: Actually, the King doesn't wear a vest. He wraps brown paper around himself. (WIZARD FUMBLE GLARES AT BORIS WHO FALLS SILENT) Sorry!

FUMBLE: (COUGHS)

But little does that mean King know,
His skinflint days are numbered,
For very soon, within this room,
By ghosties, he'll be lumbered.

BARON: You mean you will summon ghosts to frighten the King?

FUMBLE: Not frightened, are you? Then why are you both sucking your thumbs? They shan't be real ghosts. Only Bumble won't know that.

WIFE: I think that's a very silly idea, dear. The fright could give the poor man a heart attack.

BARON: Do you think there's a chance?

FUMBLE: Not a hope. The only thing that could frighten him that much was if he lost his wallet.

BORIS: But where will you get ghosts at such short notice?

FUMBLE: That's where you can help Boris.

BORIS: Me? But I don't know any ghosts. Not to speak to anyway.

FUMBLE: You misunderstand Boris. I don't want you to find a ghost for me. I want you to be one.

BORIS: Me a ghost? But don't you have to be dead first?

FX: BARON GRIME CREEPS BEHIND SIR BORIS AND PREPARES TO STRANGLE HIM

BARON: Exactly! Please don't take this personally, Boris. Just shut your eyes and think of king and country,

BORIS: Mummy!

FUMBLE: Before you do anything drastic, Baron, we need Boris' help. As I said, there aren't going to be any actual ghosts, and there aren't going to be any dead bodies, either.

FX: WIZARD FUMBLE RAPS BARON GRIME OVER THE HEAD WITH HIS WAND.

WIFE: If I were you, Fumble, I'd reconsider the whole thing. Besides, you said Bumble would be haunted in this room. Where are we going to live? In the forest?

FUMBLE: How would you like a lovely little holiday?

WIFE: A holiday, where?

FUMBLE: A castle, Bumble Castle, to be exact.

WIFE: Bumble Castle? But how?

FUMBLE: If you'll all follow me, I'll explain as I go along.

FX: WIZARD FUMBLE EXITS FOLLOWED BY THE OTHERS.

SCENE 5. INT. THE PALACE

FX:	**KING BUMBLE IS STILL SAT AT HIS TABLE WRITING IN HIS LEDGER AS THE CHANCELLOR LOOKS ON**
KING:	What is it, Chancellor? Can't you see I'm busy putting the final touches to my latest tax on luxury items?
CHANCELLOR:	Luxury items, sire?
KING:	Surely you know what luxury items are, Chancellor? Things people can do without.
CHANCELLOR:	Did you have anything particular in mind, Sire?
KING:	Yes, children.
CHANCELLOR:	Children!
KING:	Brilliant scheme, what? Destructive little blighters, children. I have two of my own, you know, Chancellor.
CHANCELLOR:	I had noticed, Sire.
KING:	This could cut vandalism at a stroke. Just think of the lovely lolly I'll be saving. For Bumblebania, of course.
CHANCELLOR:	Of course, Your Majesty. It's a truly excellent idea and very generous of you.
KING:	Generous Chancellor? You did say *generous*, didn't you?

CHANCELLOR: *Generous* was the precise word, Sire.

KING: That's what I was afraid of. I mean, that's what I thought you said. Could you explain, Chancellor?

CHANCELLOR: As Your Majesty has so accurately observed, you have two wonderful children. Therefore, in your case, the tax would be double.

KING: Double!

CHANCELLOR: Are you feeling quite well, Sire? You look a little peaky.

KING: Peaky? Me? Do I? I'm Just astonished you saw through my little jest so quickly. Ha! Ha! Tax children? I'd have to be a real old skinflint to do that now, wouldn't I? What is it you want anyway, Chancellor?

CHANCELLOR: There's someone outside who wishes an audience, Sire.

KING: He can have this one if he likes. I don't think they paid to come in.

CHANCELLOR: Very droll, Sire. (GESTURING TO A FIGURE DRESSED IN RAGS) You may enter the King's presence.

KING: (SHOCKED) Good grief! What is it, Chancellor?

CHANCELLOR: One of your subjects, Sire. I believe the correct terminology is a *peasant*.

KING: A peasant? What's a peasant?

CHANCELLOR: You know Sire. . . *"Yonder peasant, who is he? Where and what is his dwelling?"* As the Yuletide carol. . . song. . . goes.

KING: I couldn't care less where his dwelling place is or what it's made of. Just as long as he gets back to it and stays there. Pooh! What do you want, peasant? Speak up, and be quick about it.

PAGE: I'm no peasant, Sire. Don't you recognise me? It is I, Egbert, your Royal Page.

KING: Then why are you dressed in those smelly rags?

PAGE: I'm just a Page who's taken a leaf out of your book, Sire.

KING: Are you trying to be clever?

CHANCELLOR: What Egbert meant is that the clothes he's wearing are standard issue for the Royal Staff, Sire.

KING: Oh, I see. Very becoming too. I hated those silly little costumes with gold braids and bright colours. These are much more. . . more. . .

CHANCELLOR: Cheaper, Sire?

KING: Cheaper, that's it. No, it's not. Serviceable, that's the word. Well, get on with it.

PAGE: I bring you tidings, Sire, good and bad.

KING: Good news and bad news, very original. Who wrote this script anyway, Chancellor? We didn't pay him, did we?

PAGE: It concerns Sir Boris, Sire.

KING: Boris, what about Boris?

PAGE: I found him in the forest, frozen stiff, his little hands clenched around a bundle of faggots.

KING: Faggots? I didn't give him any money for faggots, or chips if it comes to that.

CHANCELLOR: Faggots are a form of fuel, Sire. You know, sticks and things.

PAGE: I'm afraid he's. . .

KING: Don't tell me. This is terrible. Did someone steal the fuel while Boris was frozen?

PAGE: Not exactly, Sire. Boris isn't with us anymore.

KING: Run away. He's a bit old for that, isn't he? Ha, ha.

CHANCELLOR: I believe he means. . . (WHISPERS IN THE KING'S EAR)

KING: Oh, I see. Well, Page, you'd better give me the bad news.

PAGE: That was the bad news, Sire.

KING: Was it? I mean, it was, of course, it was. Poor Boris. Now, what about the good news?

PAGE: How would Your Majesty like to spend the next few weeks as a guest of the P.C.H.C.?

KING: The P.C.H.C.?

PAGE: The *Peasants Country House Committee*. We have a nice centrally heated cabin available in the middle of the forest, and we, the Committee, decided to invite Your Majesty to a fortnight's free holiday. . .

KING: Free? You did say free holiday, didn't you?

PAGE: Yes Sire, absolutely free, all expenses paid.

KING: That's jolly generous of you, eh, Chancellor?

CHANCELLOR: Extremely generous, Sire.

PAGE: It's the least we could do for Your Majesty, considering everything you've done to us. . . for us.

KING: Very true. Well, Chancellor, don't just stand there. Get my suitcase packed.

CHANCELLOR: It's packed and ready, Sire, in the hallway.

KING: It is? Jolly good. I say, Chancellor, how did you know I'd need it?

CHANCELLOR: I didn't, Sire. Wishful thinking, you might say.

KING: I beg your pardon?

CHANCELLOR: I was simply hoping your actions as King would be recognised and Your Majesty would receive the reward he so justly deserves.

PAGE: You can rest assured of that, Chancellor. We'll make sure the King gets his just desserts.

KING: What a pleasant chap. Remind me to mention him in my New Year's Honours List, Chancellor.

CHANCELLOR: I doubt you'll need reminding, Sire.

KING: Probably not. Well, come on, let's not dawdle. Don't forget to put the lights out and cancel the milk, Chancellor.

FX: KING BUMBLE AND THE CHANCELLOR EXIT, FOLLOWING THE PAGE

SCENE 6. INT. WIZARD FUMBLE'S COTTAGE

FX: **THE CHANCELLOR LEADS KING BUMBLE INSIDE. THE ROOM IS IN COMPLETE DARKNESS**

CHANCELLOR: Here we are, Sire.

KING: I say, a bit dark in here, what? Put the lights on. There's a good chap.

PAGE: There are no lights, Sire.

KING: No lights?

PAGE: It's part of the charm of the place. Unspoilt, natural. . . and besides, think of all the electricity you save by not having any.

KING: I suppose you're right. At least, it sounds pretty logical, I think.

PAGE: Your Majesty must be worn out. Counting coins all day is hard work. Why don't you lie down in bed and get a good night's rest? Absolutely free of charge.

KING: Good idea. I do feel rather sleepy.

FX: **KING BUMBLE LIES DOWN AND FALLS PROMPTLY ASLEEP**

PAGE: You can come in now, Boris.

FX: **BARON GRIME ENTERS AND BECKONS TO SIR BORIS. BORIS CREEPS INTO THE ROOM. HE IS**

DRAPED IN A WHITE BLANKET FROM WHICH HIS HEAD, COVERED IN BAKING POWDER, POTRUDES.

PAGE: What's the matter, Boris? You look like you've seen a ghost.

BARON: *Been* a ghost, you mean. Ha! Ha! Ha!

BORIS: It's all very well laughing, Baron, but what if the King sees through my disguise? He's got a rotten temper, you know.

BARON: Don't worry, Boris, the worst that can happen is he'll cut your head off.

PAGE: Then you won't have to worry about a disguise.

BORIS: That's not very funny.

BARON: Oh, come on. Boris, pull yourself together. We want the king to recognise you. You're a ghost, remember?

PAGE: Shhhh! I think he's stirring.

BARON: Right, Boris, do your stuff.

FX: BARON GRIME AND EGBERT RETREAT INTO THE SHADOWS. KING BUMBLE STIRS AND SITS UP.

KING: Is someone there?

BORIS: Ooooooooooooh!

KING: Who is it? Is that you, Chancellor?

BORIS: No, it's me, Boris. . . I mean. . . the Ghost of Sir Boris the Bold.

KING: I thought you looked a bit pale. Just a shadow of the chap you were, eh, Boris? Ha! Ha! Ha! Got it, just a shadow?

BORIS: Ooooooh!

KING: Yes, of course you are. Poor chap, it must be the cold. It's petrified his brain. What you need is a bit of warming up. Nip back to the Palace and fetch my slippers. There's a good chap. A brisk jog should put the colour back in your cheeks.

BORIS: Keep away! Don't come any closer. Oooooooh!

KING: What's the matter, Boris? Upset tummy?

BORIS: Oooooooooh!

KING: You're ill, aren't you, Boris? You've got some terrible disease. Well, this is jolly inconsiderate of you, old boy. I thought we were supposed to be friends, and here you are spreading your nasty infectious germs everywhere. No thought for others, typical.

BORIS: Silence, mortal, my time is short.

KING: Short time, eh? Well, just be thankful you've got a job at all. Now, be off and fetch my slippers, or it will be the workhouse for you.

BORIS: I've come to warn you.

FX: THE KING LEAPS TO HIS FEET IN ALARM

KING: The queen's back! I knew it just when I was enjoying myself. Now, stay calm, don't panic, deep breaths.

BORIS: Not the Queen; tonight, you will be visited by three phantoms. Expect the first. . . um . . . a bit later on.

KING: Boris, stop talking rot and fetch my slippers.

PAGE: You have been warned, Sire. Oooooooooh!

FX: BORIS RETREATS INTO THE SHADOWS.

KING: Please yourself, Boris. You've had your chance. Please don't blame me when you end up in the workhouse. I hope you like gruel because that's all they serve in the soup kitchens. Old fool! Ah, well, back to bed. Phantoms indeed.

FX: KING BUMBLE CLIMBS BACK INTO BED. THREE CHIMES SOUND.

DONG! DONG! DONG!

KING: What's that? It's that infernal Palace clock. Wait a moment, I'm not in the Palace. There aren't any clocks here. What did Boris say? Phantoms. Is anybody there?

FX: A CLOAKED FIGURE ENTERS. HIS FACE CONCEALED BY A DEEP HOOD.

KING: Who, what are you? Are you a ghost?

<u>FX: THE PHANTOM NODS</u>

KING: Is it me you've come to haunt?

<u>FX: THE PHANTOM NODS</u>

KING: Why have you come?

PHANTOM: Because tonight, Ernest, Rumbleweed, Sylvester, Horatio, Bumble. . . Monarch, Founder of the Bumblebania Knights of the Square Table, Renowned Skinflint, tonight, THIS IS YOUR LIFE.

KING: My life?

PHANTOM: Surprised? They always are. Yes, tonight Ernest, Rumbleweed. . .

KING: Don't start that again; someone might hear.

PHANTOM: You can be sure of that, Horatio.

KING: What do you mean?

PHANTOM: Tonight, Sylvester, your whole life will be laid bare before this audience.

<u>FX: THE PHANTOM GESTURES TOWARDS THE AUDIENCE</u>

KING: Where did they come from?

PHANTOM: They were handpicked Bumbleweed. The most sour-faced gaggle of ghouls we could find at short notice.

FX: BUMBLE FALLS TO HIS KNEES

KING: Mercy, Phantom, I beg you, mercy.

PHANTOM: Too late, Ernest. Too late. And what do you know of mercy anyway? Do you recognise these boys?

FX: THE PHANTOM STEPS BACK INTO THE SHADOWS AS A GROUP OF BOYS ENTER ACCOMPANIED BY A GRIM-FACED TEACHER

KING: (POINTING) That's me! And there's old Smelly Smith, and that's our old teacher, Mr Hardnose. Hi, Smelly. Old chap.

PHANTOM: He cannot hear you, Bumble. He is but a shadow long past.

KING: Strange, after all these years. He's still as smelly as ever.

PHANTOM: Silence, mortal! Behold your past.

YOUNG BUMBLE: What are you crying for, Smelly?

SMELLY: Bully Briggs and his gang are after me. Unless I give them all my sweets, they're going to bash me up.

YOUNG BUMBLE: Don't worry, Smelly. I'll help you.

SMELLY: Thanks, Bumbly, you're a pal.

YOUNG BUMBLE: Give me the sweets to look after.

SMELLY: That's no good. They'll only torture me until I tell the truth. You know what they're like.

YOUNG BUMBLE: No, they won't. I'll make sure they don't get you Smelly.

SMELLY: You will?

YOUNG BUMBLE: 'Course. Now give me the sweets.

FX: SMELLY HANDS OVER THE SWEETS.

SMELLY: Here you are, Bumbly. I'll never forget this.

YOUNG BUMBLE: Sir!

HARDNOSE: What is it, Prince Bumble? Have you forgotten your homework again?

YOUNG BUMBLE: No, sir, it's Smelly Smith.

HARDNOSE: Smelly. . . master Smith. What about him?

YOUNG BUMBLE: He's been spitting in the yard again, sir.

SMELLY: But, sir!

HARDNOSE: Quiet boy! You'd better come with me.

FX: **HARDNOSE GRIPS SMELLY BY THE EAR AND LEADS HIM AWAY. YOUNG BUMBLE POPS A SWEET IN HIS MOUTH AND WATCHES THEM EXIT**

PHANTOM: Condemned by the past. Remember Bumble, "The child is father of the man." And what an odious child you were.

BUMBLE: I was, wasn't I? Mummy was always telling me how. . . what's the word?

PHANTOM: Obnoxious?

BUMBLE: That's it, obnoxious! She was always boasting about it to everybody—dear sweet Mummy.

PHANTOM: This going to be harder than I thought. Silence! Do you recall a Christmas long ago. . .a child unwrapping his solitary gift . . .

FX: **RUPERT APPEARS ON STAGE CARRYING A LARGE OBJECT WRAPPED IN CHRISTMAS PAPER.**

BUMBLE: This is a shadow of the past, isn't it Phantom?

PHANTOM: Watch and mark well.

RUPERT: Oh goody, Father Christmas came after all. Dad said he wouldn't be coming this year because he had gout. It's a big present. I bet it's the bike I asked for. I hope it's the bike. Please let it be the Acme Super-Duper Deluxe bike I asked for.

FX: **RUPERT EAGERLY RIPS THE WRAPPING PAPER TO REVEAL A LARGE EMPTY CARDBOARD BOX**

RUPERT: Boo Hoooo!

FX: **RUPERT RUNS OFF WAILING.**

PHANTOM: Are you not ashamed of your despicable behaviour?

BUMBLE: Couldn't let the boy grow up spoilt, you know. Can't bear spoilt children. I can't bear children of any kind.

PHANTOM: Then Bumble, you have something in common with your next guests. They don't like children either.

BUMBLE: They don't?

PHANTOM: Most definitely not. But they have an even greater dislike.

BUMBLE: They do, what?

PHANTOM: You! Here they come now.

FX: **A HORDE OF ANGRY VIKINGS APPEAR**

BUMBLE: Vikings! Help! Mummy!

PHANTOM: Silence! They cannot see or hear you, Bumble, which is just as well for your sake. Listen!

VIKINGS:

In days of old, we Vikings bold
Sailed oe'r the Seven Seas.
Many a town we burned to the ground

And plundered in our glee.

CHORUS

Viking men, are we

We sail the Seven Seas

We bash and smash, crush and mush,

Don’t invite us home to tea.

2

Our raven flew above the crew.

And brave men trembled when

We jumped ashore with a mighty roar

For we are Viking men.

CHORUS

Viking men, are we

We sail the Seven Seas

We bash and smash, crush and mush,

Don’t invite us home to tea.

3

One fateful day in the month of May

For Bumblebania we set sail.

With axes sharp and intent dark

We beached upon the bay.

CHORUS

Viking men, are we

We sail the Seven Seas

We bash and smash, crush and mush,

Don’t invite us home to tea.

4

We crept up to the little town

With torch in hand to burn it down.

When all at once, there came a cry

It wasn’t I, or I, or I.

A ragged crowd of children wild

Came charging down the bleak hillside.

CHORUS

Viking men, were we
We used to sail the sea
But we've been mugged
As children hugged and tugged us to the ground.

5

For little did we know
No plunder from here would go
With a King so mean
Without a bean
He'd robbed his Kingdom so.

6

No more do people fear
When we come trudging near
They laugh and shout and muck about
It's enough to make a Viking shout
And tear his cows' horns out.

7

But we'll return one day
And make that mean King pay
We'll bash and smash,
We'll crush and mush.
Bumble!
We'll get you someday.

FX: **THE VIKINGS EXIT. KING BUMBLE PEEPS OUT FROM GEHIND THE BED.**

PHANTOM: You can come out now, Bumble, they've gone.

BUMBLE: Just as well, or I would have sent them packing like I did the last time.

PHANTOM: Like *you* did Bumble?

BUMBLE: Jolly cunning of me, eh? Where would Bumblebania be without me?

PHANTOM: Bumble! Be warned. I show you now visions of things yet to pass. Unless you turn from your chosen path, Bumble, this is your future. . .

FX: A GROUP OF CHILDREN ENTER PUSHING WHAT APPEARS TO BE A SCARECROW IN A PRAM.

BUMBLE: I say it looks jolly exciting. It must be a carnival of some sort. I wonder who's paying for it?

CHILD 1: This is the best fun ever. What a party! The palace was crammed with food.

CHILD 2: Jellies!

CHILD 3: Cakes!

CHILD 4: Ice cream!

CHILD1: I feel fit to burst.

BUMBLE: Parties? The palace? There must be some mistake. Parties cost money. I hate parties.

CHILD 1: Are you going to the fireworks display tonight?

CHILD 2: Of course, isn't everyone?

CHILD 3: They are if they've any sense. It'll be the best display there's ever been. The King spent thousands.

BUMBLE: Thousands? I feel ill.

FX: A VILLAGER WANDERS PAST AND STOPS TO LOOK AT THE EFFIGY IN THE PRAM.

CHILD 4: 'Penny for the Bumble, Penny for the Bumble', mister?

VILLAGER: How can I refuse? It's the most lifelike Bumble I've ever seen. Just look at those mean, shifty eyes.

BUMBLE: How dare you!

CHILD 1: I wonder if he was as mean as they say?

CHILD 2: Worse, I'm told. He even sent his faithful friend, Sir Boris the Bold, to his death in the Frozen Forest.

CHILD 3: Not Sir Boris the Bold, the famous knight errant. The one who killed the Lesser Spotted Swamp Dragon and defeated the Black Knight single-handed?

CHILD 4: The one and the same.

CHILD 1: I'm going to enjoy burning this Bumble tonight.

CHILD 2: My Dad says it's important we don't forget what a tyrant he was.

BUMBLE: '*Tyrant*'? '*Don't forget*'? What do they mean by '*was*'?

CHILD 3: Look! Here comes the King. Hip, hip, hooray!

FX: A MUCH YOUNGER PERSON THAN KING BUMBLE ENTERS THE STAGE.

BUMBLE: Who's that? I've never seen him before in my life.

KING: (BENDING OVER TO PEER AT THE EFFIGY) What's this?

CHILD 4: It's a Bumble, Sire. We're going to burn it tonight.

KING: Oh, I see, 'Bad Old King Bumble'. He was my great-grandfather, you know.

CHILD 1: Was he really as bad as they say?

KING: Worse, in fact, your 'Bumble' flatters him. He wasn't nearly as handsome. I don't think he would have approved of all this 'waste'.

BUMBLE: Approve? I should think not! 'Bad Old Bumble' indeed.

FX: THE CHILDREN AND THE KING EXIT.

PHANTOM: Calm yourself, Bumble. These were but shadows of what might be. They have not yet come to pass.

BUMBLE: Tell me, Spirit, what must I do?

PHANTOM: At last, you see the error of your ways.

BUMBLE: I do, I do.

PHANTOM: Will you turn back from the path you have chosen?

BUMBLE: I will, I will. Only tell me what to do.

PHANTOM: Change Bumble, you must change.

BUMBLE: Change, that's it! I'll change my Will. I'll make sure that soppy great-grandson of mine doesn't get a penny. Parties, bonfires, fireworks, the boy's a spendthrift.

PHANTOM: Failed! Never before in all my years of spiriting! My time is at an end, farewell Bumble.

FX: THE PHANTOM VANISHES.

BUMBLE: Bad King Bumble, eh? Mean am I? Careful, that's what I am.

FX: PREOCCUPIED WITH HIS THOUGHTS KING BUMBLE DOES NOT NOTICE QUEEN AMMOANIA ENTER.

QUEEN: Bumble, what on earth are you doing talking to yourself?

BUMBLE: Go away. I'm busy. I've had enough phantoms for one night.

QUEEN: Phantoms! I knew I shouldn't have left you on your own. You're quite hopeless.

BUMBLE: Ammoania beloved, is it really you?

QUEEN: Of course, it's me; whatever is the matter with you, Bumble? Why on earth are you staying in this hovel?

BUMBLE: I was offered. . .

QUEEN: Don't interrupt, Bumble. I couldn't believe it when the Chancellor told me where you were.

BUMBLE: The Chancellor?

QUEEN: Come along. I can't stand around here listening to you prattling on all night. Rupert is waiting for us in the palace.

BUMBLE: Rupert?

QUEEN: Surely you remember Rupert, Bumble, your son? He absolutely refuses to go to bed until he sees what you've bought him for Christmas.

BUMBLE: He doesn't? I didn't expect you back until. . .

QUEEN: The New Year, I know. I couldn't let you spend Christmas alone; that would have been too selfish of me. I know what Christmas means to you, Bumble, dear.

BUMBLE: Christmas? Yes, of course,

QUEEN: You can tell me about the preparations on the way back.

BUMBLE: Preparations?

QUEEN: Don't be dense, Bumble. The Christmas preparations, parties. . . presents. . . the turkey dinner.

FX: THE QUEEN EXITS WITH BUMBLE TRAILING FORLORNLY BEHIND. SIR BORIS AND BARON GRIME EMERGE FROM THEIR HIDING PLACE.

BORIS: That was a jolly close call.

BARON: Poor old Bumble. One could almost feel sorry for him. Almost!

BORIS: I say, Wizard Fumble came up trumps this time. This must be the best trick he's pulled in years.

BARON: It certainly was. I don't know how he did it. What's that?

<u>FX: A SUDDEN NOISE STARTLES THE PAIR WHO GRASP EACH OTHER'S HAND. WIZARD FUMBLE AND HIS WIFE ENTER.</u>

BORIS: Wizard Fumble!

BARON: Let go of my hand, Boris.

FUMBLE: It's too late. We'll have to call it off. The Queen is back.

BORIS: Call it off, but. . .

FUMBLE: She arrived back unexpectedly. Mrs Fumble and I had to escape through the window.

WIFE: That's the last time I'm shinning down drainpipes for anyone, Fumble.

BARON: But you were here.

FUMBLE: What are you talking about, Baron? We were miles away trying to dodge the Queen.

WIFE: Don't remind me, Fumble. We had to hide in the trees while you pair were dozing by our fire.

FUMBLE: There, there, beloved.

WIFE: Don't '*beloved*' me. I'm fed up with your crackpot spells. I'm off home to mother.

FX: MRS FUMBLE STOMPS OFF.

BARON: But if it wasn't you, Fumble, who was it?

FUMBLE: Who was what?

FX: THE PHANTOM REAPPEARS.

BORIS: Him!

FUMBLE: Him?

BARON: Him.

ALL THREE: Aaaaaaaah!

FX: BORIS, FUMBLE AND THE BARON EXIT HEADLONG THROUGH THE DOOR.

PHANTOM: (BOWING TO AUDIENCE) A Merry and a Blessed Christmas to you all.

FX: HE TURNS AND EXITS.

END

More Chronicles of Bumblebania:

Christmas At Bumble Castle

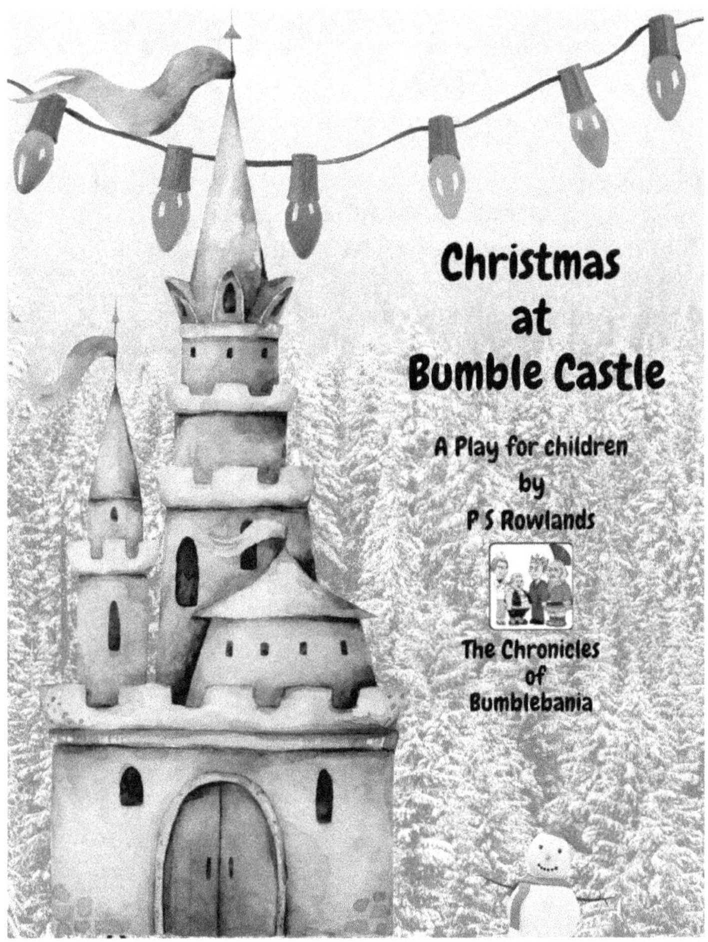

Christmas is coming, and the Royal House of Bumble is in turmoil. While the King and Sir Boris the Bold set about restoring the Ancient Order of Knighthood, Queen Ammoania is feverishly attempting to find a suitor for the princess.
Meanwhile, having escaped from the clutches of Prince Rupert and his gang, dastardly Baron Grime hatches a fiendishly clever plot that is in danger of coming undone, literally.

When an Abominable Snowman is sighted in Bumblebania and Aunt Grimwalda arrives unannounced for the wedding, it seems that things cannot get any worse.

But they can.

Visit: www.talesfromwales.net

THE SCIENCE DRAMA PLAY SCRIPTS

Five award-winning Science Drama Play Scripts.

Sherlock Ohms and the Mystery of Magnet Manor

Theme: Electricity

When Sherlock Ohms is summoned to Magnet Manor by the mysterious A. T. Mos he senses devilry afoot. His suspicions are further aroused upon learning that five of the wealthiest men in the world have also received similar invitations. Accompanied by his loyal companion Dr Watts-On he travels to the remote island unaware of the tragic events that will shortly unfold.
As the guests fall victim to the evil A. T. Mos, one by one, can Ohms solve the mystery and uncover the evil perpetrator before no one is left standing?

Birdflight

Theme: Migration

Young Redstart is discovering what a dangerous world he inhabits. Old Crow tells him tales of fearsome creatures like Sparrowhawk, Stoat, and the deadly Pine Marten, who once hunted through the trees like a dark shadow. Yet there is one danger he cannot escape. A danger he must face with family and friends afresh each year or perish when the freezing white death descends upon the land. Is he ready to undertake the great adventure of migration?

Slime
Theme: Pollution and the Ecology of a Pond
Why has the pond suddenly become plagued with frogs? Are the rumours of the deadly black slime true? Will Pond Snail escape the clutches of Mr and Mrs Water Spider? Can the Tadpoles trust Great Diving Beetle? What happened to Kingfisher? Can they all escape the deadly black slime?

This Was Your Life
THEME: The Global Ecological Crisis
Every week, our television screens are filled with scenes of fresh disasters – famine, earthquakes, floods and deadly forest fires. As we watch from the comfort of our sofas, what if, one day, the face peering back at us was our own?

Steam
THEME: The Steam Engine and the Industrial Revolution
John Williams was born in the rural village of Cowbridge, South Wales, in 1815 and died in a locomotive accident on the Rhondda Valley Railway in 1865. His life encompassed the dawn of the Industrial Revolution. This is his story and of the men who helped change the world.

www.ingramcontent.com/pod-product-compliance
Lightning Source LLC
LaVergne TN
LVHW080818170826
845678LV00011B/2065

* 9 7 8 1 7 3 9 1 3 6 0 4 8 *